D0975316

So,
now you
know. . .

A Compendium of
Completely Useless
Information

HARRY BRIGHT
&
HARLAN BRISCOE

MJF BOOKS
New York

Published by MJF Books
Fine Communications
322 Eighth Avenue
New York, NY 10001

So, Now You Know…
ISBN-13: 978-1-56731-693-3
ISBN-10: 1-56731-693-X
Library of Congress Number 2004108692

MV   12   11   10   9   8   7   6   5

So, Now You Know . . .

THE answer to the age-old question of which came first, the chicken or the egg, can be found in the Bible.

GENESIS 1:20–22

THE Bible is available in nearly 2,500 languages, including Klingon, Vulcan, and Romulan, three languages created for the *Star Trek* series.

THE name for the search engine Google is derived from the word *googol*, which refers to the number 1 followed by one hundred zeros.

$$\begin{array}{r} 111{,}111{,}111 \\ \times \ 111{,}111{,}111 \\ \hline 12{,}345{,}678{,}987{,}654{,}321 \end{array}$$

a palindromic number.

IF the DNA in all your cells were laid out in a single strand, it would stretch from the earth to the moon more than 246,000 times.

On six-sided dice, the opposite sides always add up to seven.

THE muzzle of a lion is like a fingerprint—no two lions have the same pattern of whiskers.

Genetically speaking, zebras are black with white stripes, not white with black stripes; they have black skin, even under the white hair.

GIRAFFES and humans have the same number of vertebrae in the neck—seven; the giraffes' are just much larger.

On March 29, 1848, the Niagara River froze solid, stopping the flow of the tremendous Niagara Falls. For a few hours, locals were able to walk along the riverbed upon which the falls cascade.

THE largest desert on Earth is in Antarctica. It covers an area of more than 5.4 million square miles, over one and one-half times larger than the Sahara Desert.

NINETY percent of the world's ice is in Antarctica, though precipitation there averages only two inches per year.

IF the entire population of China were to walk past you in single file, you would not live long enough to see the end of the line.

THE driest place on Earth is Calama, a town in the Atacama Desert of northern Chile, which has no recorded rainfall.

THE world's least populated country is Vatican City, which has roughly 1,000 residents.

WATER exists on the sun. Studies by an international team of scientists recorded evidence of water, in the form of vapor or steam, in the sun's dark sunspots. At a mere 4,760°F–5,300°F, the darkest part of a sunspot is one of the coolest areas of the sun's surface. At temperatures higher than 8,540°F, water becomes unstable and splits into oxygen and hydrogen.

A black hole in the Perseus galaxy cluster, about 250 million light-years from Earth, emits sound waves with a frequency of about 10 million years, making them the lowest notes in the universe. The sound, a B-flat fifty-seven octaves lower than middle C, is generally considered to be a cheerful one, although it cannot be heard by the human ear.

PEPSI-COLA was invented by a young pharmacist named Caleb Bradham in 1898. Originally called "Brad's Drink," the beverage was first marketed as a digestive aid and energy booster; it was renamed Pepsi-Cola because of its pepsin and kola nut content.

GORE-TEX, the breathable composite polymer used to waterproof and windproof outdoor gear, is simply stretched Teflon, the substance used to coat nonstick pans.

THE modern image of Santa Claus as a rosy-cheeked old man wearing a plush red suit was popularized by American artist Haddon Sundblom in advertisements for the Coca-Cola Company in the 1930s. Coca-Cola hit upon this advertising campaign as a way to boost slumping sales during the winter months of the Great Depression.

BARNUM'S ANIMALS (commonly known as Animal Crackers) were first produced with a string on the box so they could be used as Christmas tree ornaments.

IN the mid-1800s, famous French trapeze artist Jules Léotard began wearing skintight bodysuits, which made it easier to perform his stunts. The bodysuits became so associated with Léotard that the name stuck.

GEORGE WASHINGTON

rejected a movement among army officers to make him king of the United States, saying, "I didn't fight George III to become George I."

WASHINGTON was the first president under the U.S. Constitution of 1789, but he was actually America's *eighth* president. Before the Constitution was ratified, a new country had been formed on March 1, 1781, with the adoption of the Articles of Confederation; seven men served as president under these Articles.

THE presidential elections of 1876 and 2000 both ended in a deadlock, with Florida's electoral votes in dispute. In both elections, partisan Florida Republicans gave the state's electoral votes to the Republican candidate, and Democrats challenged the result. Both challenges were decided by a single vote cast by a Republican Supreme Court justice in favor of the Republicans.

MILLIE'S BOOK, the "auto-biography" of former president George H. W. Bush's White House dog, was published in 1991; the book earned nearly $900,000 in royalties—more than four times the $200,000 salary George Bush Sr. earned as president that year!

MILLIE gave birth to President George W. Bush's dog Spot at the White House on March 17, 1989. The friendly brown-and-white spaniel is the only second-generation presidential pet in history.

THE basenji is the only breed of dog that doesn't bark—it yodels.

BRITISH merchant Peter Durand came up with the idea of canned food in 1810, but the can opener wasn't invented until forty-eight years later. Before Ezra J. Warner patented the first can opener in 1858, cans were opened with a hammer and chisel.

THE introduction of the traffic light predated the invention of the automobile.

In 1896 Svante Arrhenius, the Nobel Prize–winning Swedish chemist, was the first to predict global warming when he suggested that burning fossil fuels would result in the buildup of carbon dioxide in the earth's atmosphere.

ACCORDING to a United Nations University study, roughly 1.8 tons of raw materials are required to manufacture the average desktop PC and monitor—528 pounds of fossil fuels, 48 pounds of chemicals, and 3,300 pounds of water. The total amount of materials used is about equal to the weight of a midsize car.

IN England, the Speaker of the House is not allowed to speak; his main responsibility is to preside over the deliberations.

ALL swans in England
are the property of the queen.

RAVENS are kept in the Tower of London, and, according to myth, the British throne will fall if they leave. Not surprisingly, the British government clips the ravens' wings to prevent them from flying away.

THERE are more plastic flamingos than real ones in the United States. Designed by Don Featherstone, more than 20 million plastic pink flamingos have been sold since 1957.

PINK flamingos get their color from the beta-carotene content in the shrimp they eat. Flamingos that don't eat shrimp are white, not pink.

A group of flamingos is called a pat. A group of frogs is called an army. A group of rhinoceroses is called a crash. A group of kangaroos is called a mob. A group of apes is called a shrewdness. A group of cats is called a clutter. A group of larks is called an exaltation. A group of owls is called a parliament. A group of ravens is called a murder.

A baby beaver is a kit. A baby codfish is a sprat. A baby elephant seal is a weaner. A baby fish is a fry. A baby frog is a polliwog. A baby kangaroo is a joey. A baby swan is a cygnet. A baby tiger is a whelp. A baby shark is a cub.

A hive of bees must pollinate 2 million flowers to make one pound of honey, requiring them to fly an equivalent distance of approximately 55,000 miles—or more than twice around the globe.

MALE bees, or drones, have only one job—to mate with the queen. Those lucky enough to do so die in the act.

TIME magazine's "Man of the Year" for 1938 was Adolf Hitler.

Hitler's private train was called "Amerika."

THROUGHOUT World War II, Hitler was administered daily injections of methamphetamine, an addictive stimulant commonly known today as speed.

Aт the time of Pearl Harbor, the top U.S. Navy command was called CINCUS (pronounced "sink us").

A natural instinct in mammals causes their hackles to rise when they are alarmed or frightened. While human beings no longer have thick coats of hair, they still have muscles that raise tiny bumps on the flesh, known as goose bumps.

ABSOLUTE zero, the temperature at which all motion ceases, is -460°F.

IF you are sailing in the Strait of Messina and come upon a castle floating in thin air, you are seeing an optical illusion called a *fata morgana*, which only occurs where there are alternating warm and cold layers of air rising from the surface.

At latitude 60° south it is possible to sail clear around the world without touching land.

On average, in any given hour there are 61,000 people airborne over the United States.

Aaccording to the U.S. Transportation Security Administration, in 2003 passengers left $303,970 in loose change at airport metal detectors. The U.S. Treasury Department appropriates the money and returns it to circulation.

A report introduced in the U.S. Senate states that a child will have witnessed 8,000 murders and 100,000 acts of violence on television before completing elementary school.

IN 1972 the FBI hired its first two female agents: a former nun and a former U.S. marine.

THE tombstone of Mel Blanc, the famed voice of cartoon characters Bugs Bunny, Sylvester the Cat, Tweety Bird, and Porky Pig, reads: "That's all folks."

IN 1980, thirty-one years after the Road Runner cartoons debuted, in an episode titled "Soup or Sonic," Wile E. Coyote finally catches the Road Runner; he then holds up a sign saying, "Okay, wise guys, you always wanted me to catch him. Now what do I do?"

STEVE HILLENBURG created the Nickelodeon cartoon *SpongeBob SquarePants*, the story of a yellow sea sponge who lives in a pineapple at the bottom of the Pacific Ocean with his pet snail, Gary; Hillenburg got his inspiration for the idea while working as a marine science educator.

NAMED after the Pulitzer Prize–winning cartoonist, a Rube Goldberg machine is any exceedingly complex apparatus that performs a very simple task in a very indirect and convoluted way.

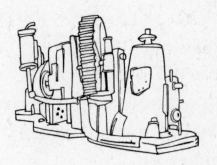

IN 1946 Walt Disney Studios produced an animated educational film titled *The Story of Menstruation* in conjunction with the manufacturer of Kotex feminine pads.

CHOCOLATE syrup was used for blood in the famous 45-second shower scene in Alfred Hitchcock's movie *Psycho*; the scene actually took seven days to shoot.

Months that begin on a Sunday will always have a Friday the 13th.

TRISKAIDEKAPHOBIA means "fear of the number thirteen." The superstitious belief that thirteen is an unlucky number comes from Judas Iscariot's betrayal of Christ at the Last Supper, when the twelve apostles and Jesus were gathered together for the last time.

THE term *devil's advocate* comes from the Roman Catholic Church; when deciding if someone should be sainted, the Church appoints a devil's advocate to give an alternate view.

THERE is no recorded date of Christ's birth. Christmas became an official church holiday in AD 320; Pope Julius I chose December 25 in an effort to absorb the customs of the pagan festival Saturnalia, an extended hedonistic holiday marking the winter solstice, during which the normal Roman social order was turned upside down.

THOUGH the crescent moon and star can be found on the flag of many Islamic countries, it is not an official symbol of Islam. According to the *Hadith*, a collection of sayings and acts of Muhammad and early Muslims, it is a sin to use anything as a symbol of Allah.

T HERE are no permanent rivers or lakes in Saudi Arabia.

RATU UDRE UDRE, a
nineteenth-century Fijian chief,
holds the Guinness World Record
for "most prolific cannibal";
he reportedly ate between
872 and 999 people.

An exocannibal eats only his enemies while an indocannibal eats only his friends.

THE hottest place on Earth is the air around a lightning strike, which can reach as much as 54,000°F, easily five times hotter than the surface of the sun.

Lightning strikes about 6,000 times per minute on this planet.

A tropical storm must have wind speeds in excess of 39 miles per hour before it is assigned a name, and it is officially classified as a hurricane when sustained wind speeds reach 74 miles per hour.

IN ten minutes, a hurricane releases more energy than all the world's nuclear weapons detonated at once.

Terrorism was originally defined in the Oxford English Dictionary as "government by intimidation."

THE term *weapons of mass destruction* was coined in 1937 to describe aerial bombings in the Spanish Civil War.

SOLDIERS in the American Civil War needed at least two opposing front teeth to rip open gunpowder envelopes. Some men called up for induction had their front teeth extracted to avoid military service.

JELLYBEANS did not become an Easter tradition until the 1930s. They were first made in America by Boston candy maker William Schrafft, who ran advertisements urging people to send jellybeans to soldiers fighting in the Civil War.

Tootsie Rolls were introduced in 1896 by Leo Hirshfield; he named them after his daughter, whose nickname was "Tootsie."

THE Snickers bar, introduced in 1930 by M&M/Mars, is named after the Mars family's favorite horse, Snickers.

IN 1920 the first "Baby Ruth" candy bar was sold. It is named after President Grover Cleveland's daughter—not the legendary baseball player Babe Ruth.

BABE RUTH wore a cabbage leaf under his baseball cap to keep cool; he changed it every two innings.

Ａccording to a representative of the Rawlings Sporting Goods Company, official supplier to Major League Baseball, the average life span of a major league baseball is just six pitches.

THE English invented football—known in America as soccer—when they kicked around the heads of Danish invaders they had slaughtered.

THE American football is referred to as a "pigskin" because footballs were originally made of pigs' bladders wrapped in pigskin.

IT takes more than 2,000 cows to supply the NFL with enough leather for a year's worth of footballs.

ABE LINCOLN'S mother died from drinking the milk of the family dairy cow after it had eaten poisonous mushrooms.

ICE CREAM dates back to the second century BC, when Alexander the Great enjoyed snow and ice flavored with honey and nectar.

THE first American ice-cream parlor opened in New York City in 1776.

Edy's Grand Ice Cream created the flavor Rocky Road after the stock market crash of October 1929. The company hoped the flavor's whimsical name would give people something to smile about.

RATS can have sex twenty times per day. They multiply so quickly that one pair of rats might have more than 15,000 descendants in a year.

EXPERTS estimate that there are more than 56 million rats in New York City, or roughly seven rats for every person.

BOTANICALLY speaking, the banana is an herb, the jalapeño is a fruit, and apples and peaches are members of the rose family.

P

INEAPPLES, oranges, lemons, watermelons, and tomatoes are all berries.

T̲HE strawberry is the only fruit with seeds on the outside of the skin.

EATING celery actually burns calories; the calories are burned in the digestion process, not by chewing.

THE science-fiction television series *Lost in Space*, which premiered on CBS in 1965, is set in the year 1997.

IN the film *Raiders of the Lost Ark*, when Indiana Jones falls into a snake pit in Egypt, there is an image hidden among the wall's hieroglyphics of C-3PO and R2-D2, robots in the *Star Wars* movies.

BELLE, from Disney's animated film *Beauty and the Beast*, can be glimpsed in a crowd scene in another Disney animated feature, *The Hunchback of Notre Dame*.

Seeking a sage and wizened look, the creators of *Star Wars* modeled Yoda's face after Albert Einstein.

LEONARDO DA VINCI could write with one hand and draw with the other simultaneously. He always wrote backward so that one could only read his writing with a mirror.

THE most expensive book ever sold at auction was da Vinci's *The Codex Leicester*—his observations and illustrations on natural phenomena; the book was sold on November 11, 1994, to software magnate Bill Gates for $30.8 million.

DA VINCI'S *Mona Lisa* has no eyebrows, following the fashion for women in Renaissance Florence to completely pluck their eyebrows. Her famous, close-mouthed smile may be meant to hide rotten teeth.

IN the movie *Casablanca*, Rick never says, "Play it again, Sam." It is Ilsa who says, "Play it, Sam. Play 'As Time Goes By.'"

IN the early days of filmmaking, the people working the sets were called movies and the films were called motion pictures.

IN the Mel Brooks comedy *Silent Movie*, world-famous mime Marcel Marceau has the only speaking role.

ONE of the "Bond girls" appearing in the 1981 film *For Your Eyes Only* is a transsexual; she is listed in the credits as "Girl at Pool."

Actress Sharon Stone's first role in a feature film was a cameo in Woody Allen's 1980 comedy, *Stardust Memories*. She is credited only as "Pretty Girl on Train."

ACCORDING to a study published in the *International Journal of Eating Disorders*, by Yale University professor Kelly Brownell, PhD, if the original Barbie were life-size, her measurements would be 38-18-34 and she would stand seven feet, two inches tall.

CINDERELLA's slippers were originally made of fur. The story was inadvertently changed by a translator in the 1600s, who confused the very similar old French words for "glass" and "fur"—*verre* and *vair*, respectively.

THE unpopped kernels in a bowl of popcorn are called "old maids."

HOLLYWOOD legend has it that in 1931 executive director of the Academy of Arts and Sciences, Margaret Herrick, dubbed the Academy Award statuette "Oscar" because she thought it resembled her uncle Oscar.

More than 63 million times each day, AOL users sign on and hear voice-over actor Elwood Edwards say the words, "You've got mail!"

JACK NICHOLSON appeared on *The Andy Griffith Show* twice, in 1966 and 1967.

THE title role of *Dirty Harry* (1971) was originally intended for Frank Sinatra. After Sinatra refused, it was offered to John Wayne, and then Paul Newman, and was finally accepted by Clint Eastwood.

KELSEY GRAMMAR sings and plays the piano for the theme song of *Frasier*.

The "think music" for
Jeopardy's final round was written
by the show's creator,
Merv Griffin.

THE CBS news magazine *60 Minutes* is the only television show that does not have a theme song. The intense ticking of a stopwatch suffices as the show's trademark theme.

THE first toilet ever shown on television appeared in 1957, in an episode of *Leave It to Beaver*, titled "Captain Jack."

Dentists have recommended storing a toothbrush at least six feet away from a toilet to avoid contact with airborne particles resulting from the flush.

THE electric chair was invented in 1881 by a dentist, Albert Southwick; Southwick maintained that electrocution was a more humane method of execution than hanging after witnessing an elderly drunkard "painlessly" killed after touching the terminals of an electrical generator in Buffalo, New York.

BULLETPROOF vests, fire escapes, and windshield wipers were all invented by women.

HELEN KELLER was a founding member of the American Civil Liberties Union (ACLU).

ONE in three Americans bite their fingernails.

THE white area at the base of the fingernail is called the *lunula* because it resembles a crescent moon.

IF you want to lose weight, weigh yourself when there's a full moon—you'll weigh less.

Roughly 12 percent of all workers in the United States have at some point worked at a McDonald's restaurant.

With the introduction of the Happy Meal, McDonald's became the largest toy distributor in the world.

McDonald's restaurants in India do not serve beef—only chicken, mutton, and fish.

IN May 1997, 32-year-old Phoenix resident Dale Novak won the SPAM-carving contest with his creation of a small SPAM castle, appropriately dubbed "Spamalot."

THE heart of a full-grown blue whale is the size of a small car; its tongue is as long as an elephant.

THE Alaskan wood frog survives long, bitter Arctic winters by turning into a "frogsicle": It becomes frozen solid, and for several months its heart stops beating and it doesn't draw a single breath. When the weather warms, the frog miraculously thaws and comes back to life.

Wɪᴛʜ just one shock, an electric eel produces enough energy to light up every room in an average three-bedroom house.

THE first singing telegram issued by Western Union was delivered by an operator named Lucille Lipps to American vocalist Rudy Vallee on July 28, 1933, in honor of his thirty-second birthday. She sang "Happy Birthday to You."

The song "Happy Birthday to You" was originally written by sisters Mildred and Patty Hill as "Good Morning to You"; the words were changed when it was published in 1935. Annual royalties for the song average $2 million.

Swedish chemist and inventor Alfred Nobel left his estate to endow annual prizes for those who have conferred the greatest benefit to humanity, now known as Nobel Prizes; Nobel made his fortune by inventing the highly destructive explosive dynamite.

Since 1991, bona fide Nobel laureates have handed out Ig Nobel Prizes. The brainchild of Marc Abrahams, editor of *Annals of Improbable Research*, Igs are awarded for "achievements that cannot or should not be reproduced." Past winners include a team of Australian scientists who conducted "An Analysis of the Forces Required to Drag Sheep over Various Surfaces" and a paper from Stockholm entitled "Chickens Prefer Beautiful Humans."

ROBIN WILLIAMS, Tom Cruise, Gene Hackman, and Dr. Seuss were all voted "Least Likely to Succeed" by their classmates.

COMEDIAN Jerry Lewis is the only entertainer on record to be nominated for the Nobel Peace Prize (1977); his nomination was parodied in a November 2003 episode of *The Simpsons*.

THE SIMPSONS creator, Matt Groening, named the characters Homer, Marge, Lisa, and Maggie after his real-life father, mother, and two sisters. The Simpsons' hometown of Springfield is named after Groening's hometown of Springfield, Oregon.

In his will, Shakespeare left his wife his "second best bed."

IN Shakespeare's time, mattresses were secured on bed frames by ropes. Pulling on the ropes tightened the mattress and made it firmer; hence the expression "Goodnight, sleep tight."

CIMEX LECTULARIUS, commonly known as the bed bug, is capable of consuming its body weight in blood in five minutes.

DISEASES spread by fleas have killed more people than all the wars ever fought, combined.

THE worst plague of all time— that is, the one that killed the most people in the shortest period of time—was not the bubonic plague of the fourteenth century; it was the Spanish Flu pandemic of 1918–1919, which took more than 20 million lives in a matter of months.

I<small>T</small>'s very beautiful over there"
were Thomas Edison's last words,
which he uttered after briefly
coming out of a two-day coma
before passing away.

THE Coca-Cola Company purchases more sugar than any other company in the world. Besides being a liquid refreshment, Coca-Cola is commonly used to clean toilets, remove rust, baste ham, and dissolve driveway grease.

COLA-FLAVORED JELL-O was introduced in 1942, but flopped and was discontinued within a year; other failed JELL-O flavors include celery, chocolate, coffee, and apple.

POP TARTS, introduced on September 14, 1964, were named as a pun on "pop art."

YOUNG female pop music artists with a provocative fashion sense are now referred to as "pop tarts."

BOTH Kellogg's Corn Flakes and Graham Crackers were originally marketed as remedies for chronic masturbation.

THE pharmaceutical company Pfizer Inc. sells about nine Viagra pills every second. Before this "little blue pill" became one of the most recognizable prescription drugs ever, it was a bust as a treatment for hypertension and angina. The scientists at Pfizer were ready to give up on the drug when they observed an unusual side effect during a toleration study.

SYNESTHESIA is a rare condition in which stimuli to one sense are perceived by other senses. Synesthetes can smell words, taste colors, or even see music.

A Valentine's Day party in Victorian times would find young ladies writing their name on slips of paper. The young men would draw a slip and pin it to their sleeve, which is where the expression "Wearing your heart on your sleeve" comes from.

MEDIEVAL Italians came up with the idea of giving diamond engagement rings to prospective brides.

WEDDING rings derive from the ancient Egyptian custom of placing ring-money (rings used as money) on the bride's finger to indicate that she was endowed with her husband's wealth.

IN the sixteenth and seventeenth centuries it was fashionable to wear one's wedding ring on the thumb.

A poem written in honor of a bride and bridegroom is called an *epithalamium*.

FRANCIS SCOTT KEY wrote the poem "The Star Spangled Banner" during the War of 1812. The poem attained wide popularity when sung to the tune of "To Anacreon in Heaven," a traditional British drinking song; it was officially named the U.S. national anthem in 1931.

THE song "Rudolph, the Red-Nosed Reindeer" was created in 1939 in Chicago as a Christmas promotion for the Montgomery Ward department stores. The lyrics were written as a poem by Robert May, and weren't set to music until 1947; Gene Autry recorded the hit song in 1949.

THE motto of the United States Postal Service—"Neither snow nor rain nor heat nor gloom of night stays these couriers from the swift completion of their appointed rounds"—was supplied by the architectural firm that built the central post office building in New York City. The quote was adapted from an original line by Greek historian Herodotus (484?–425? BC).

Your feet are bigger in the afternoon than they are during the rest of the day; this is due to blood pooling.

The apparatus for measuring feet at a shoe store is a Brannock device.

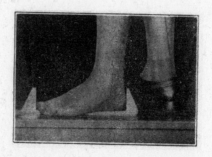

MARK TWAIN (pseudonym of Samuel Langhorne Clemens) was born November 30, 1835, the year Haley's Comet passed over the earth. He vowed he would not die until he saw the famous comet for himself; he died the day after it passed over the earth in 1910.

COUNTRY music icon Shania Twain was born Eilleen Regina Edwards; in 1990 she adopted her current name, a Native American Chippewa (or Ojibwa) phrase meaning "I'm on my way."

BIRTH NAME

Cher . . . . Cherilyn Sarkisian

Chuck Norris . . . . . . Carlos Ray

Enya . . . . Eithne Ni Bhraonian

Hulk Hogan . . . . . . Terry Jean Bollette

Ice-T . . . . Tracy Morrow

Meat Loaf . . . . Marvin Lee Aday

Queen Latifah . . . . . Dana Owens

Robert Blake . . . . Michael James
Vijencio Gubitosi

Stevie Wonder . . . . . Stevland Morris

Tom Cruise . . . . Thomas Mapothrer IV

Whoopi Goldberg . . Caryn Johnson

FRENCH sculptor Frédéric Bartholdi's original design for the Statue of Liberty, called "Egypt Carrying the Light of Asia," was intended to be placed in Port Said, Egypt, to commemorate the completion of the Suez Canal.

ANCIENT Egyptians regarded a tattoo as a sign of wealth.

THE dot over the letter *i* is called a *tittle*. *Tittle* also means "iota" or "little bit," as in, "I don't care one tittle."

A "jiffy" is an actual unit of time, most commonly interpreted as 1/100th of a second.

THE origin of the word *trivia* comes from the Latin *tri*, meaning "three," and *via*, meaning "street." The Latin word *trivium* means "public square," where the ancient Romans would gather to discuss everyday things.

THE phrase "It ain't over till the fat lady sings" is derived from earlier versions, such as "The opera isn't over until the fat lady sings" and "Church ain't out till the fat lady sings." Dan Cook, a sportscaster in San Antonio, Texas, is credited with popularizing the current version in 1978 when he said it on national television during the NBA playoffs, after the San Antonio Spurs went down three games to one against the Washington Bullets.